*

*I will give to you
the keys of the Kingdom of Heaven*

(Matthew 16, 19)

*

*For we are made partakers of Christ,
if we hold the beginning of our confidence
stedfast unto the end.*

(Hebrews 3, 14)

*

The Healing Miracles of Jesus

Healing Miracles of the Apostles

and a Message to all Believers

Bibliografische Information der Deutschen Nationalbibliothek:
Die Deutsche Nationalbibliothek verzeichnet diese Publikation in der Deutschen Nationalbibliografie: detaillierte bibliografische Daten sind im Internet über http://dnb.dnb.de abrufbar.

TWENTYSIX
Eine Marke der Books on Demand GmbH

Herstellung und Verlag:
BoD – Books on Demand, Norderstedt

ISBN: 978-3-740-78189-7

Translation: **King James Version**

Layout, Schriftsatz, Formatierung:
Antonia Katharina Tessnow
www.antonia-katharina.de

Content

Who is Jesus - the Healing Miracles of Jesus	9
The Command of Jesus to his Disciples - Our Mission in the World	78
Healing Miracles of the Apostles	86
The Power of God, working through Jesus	98
The Faith that moves Mountains	102

We, the Labourers in the Name of Jesus Christ

A Message - not only to the Apostles, but also to us	106
The Promise of an Answer to Prayer	110
A Reminder to the Readers to live a Life according to their Calling	112
A Request regarding your Behavior towards one Another	114

Register	118
Thanks	120
About the Author	122
Further Publications	123

Verily, verily, I say unto you,
He that believeth on me,
the works that I do
shall he do also

.

(John 14, 12)

Who is Jesus?

John 1, 1 – 41

In the beginning was the Word, and the Word was with God, and the Word was God. The same was in the beginning with God. All things were made by him; and without him was not any thing made that was made.

In him was life; and the life was the light of men. And the light shineth in darkness; and the darkness comprehended it not.

There was a man sent from God, whose name was John. The same came for a witness, to bear witness of the Light, that all men through him might believe. He was not that Light, but was sent to bear witness of that Light.

That was the true Light, which lighteth every man that cometh into the world. He was in the world, and the world was made by him, and the world knew him not.

He came unto his own, and his own received him not. But as many as received him, to them gave he power to become the sons of God, even to them that believe on his name; which were born, not of blood, nor of the will of the flesh, nor of the will of man, but of God.

And the Word was made flesh, and dwelt among us, (and we beheld his glory, the glory as of the only begotten of the Father, full of grace and truth.

John bare witness of him, and cried, saying, This was he of whom I spake, He that cometh after me is preferred before me; for he was before me.

And of his fulness have all we received, and grace for grace. For the law was given by Moses, but grace and truth came by Jesus Christ.

No man hath seen God at any time, the only begotten Son, which is in the bosom of the Father, he hath declared him.

And this is the record of John, when the Jews sent priests and Levites from Jerusalem to ask him, Who art thou?

And he confessed, and denied not; but confessed, I am not the Christ.

And they asked him, What then? Art thou Elias?

And he saith, I am not.

Art thou that prophet?

And he answered, No.

Then said they unto him, Who art thou? that we may give an answer to them that sent us. What sayest thou of thyself?

He said, I am the voice of one crying in the wilderness, Make straight the way of the Lord, as said the prophet Esaias.

And they which were sent were of the Pharisees. And they asked him, and said unto him, Why baptizest thou then, if thou be not that Christ, nor Elias, neither that prophet?

John answered them, saying, I baptize with water; but there standeth one among you, whom ye know not; He it is, who coming after me is preferred before me, whose shoe's latchet I am not worthy to unloose.

These things were done in Bethabara beyond Jordan, where John was baptizing.

The next day John seeth Jesus coming unto him, and saith, Behold the Lamb of God, which taketh away the sin of the world. This is he of whom I said, After me cometh a man which is preferred before me; for he was before me. And I knew him not; but that he should be made manifest to Israel, therefore am I come baptizing with water.

And John bare record, saying, I saw the Spirit descending from heaven like a dove, and it abode upon him. And I knew him not; but he that sent me to baptize with water, the same said unto me, Upon whom thou shalt see the Spirit descending, and remaining on him, the same is he which baptizeth with the Holy Ghost. And I saw, and bare record that this is the Son of God.

Again the next day after John stood, and two of his disciples; And looking upon Jesus as he walked, he saith, Behold the Lamb of God!

And the two disciples heard him speak, and they followed Jesus. Then Jesus turned, and saw them following, and saith unto them, What seek ye?

They said unto him, Rabbi, (which is to say, being interpreted, Master,) where dwellest thou?

He saith unto them, Come and see.

They came and saw where he dwelt, and abode with him that day; for it was about the tenth hour. One of the two which heard John speak, and followed him, was Andrew, Simon Peter's brother. He first findeth his own brother Simon, and saith unto him, We have found the Messias, which is, being interpreted, the Christ.

Healing of an Possessed in the Synagoge of Capernaum

Mark 1, 21 - 28

And they went into Capernaum; and straightway on the sabbath day he entered into the synagogue, and taught. And they were astonished at his doctrine; for he taught them as one that had authority, and not as the scribes.

And there was in their synagogue a man with an unclean spirit; and he cried out, saying, Let us alone; what have we to do with thee, thou Jesus of Nazareth? art thou come to destroy us? I know thee who thou art, the Holy One of God.

And Jesus rebuked him, saying, Hold thy peace, and come out of him.

And when the unclean spirit had torn him, and cried with a loud voice, he came out of him. And they were all amazed, insomuch that they questioned among themselves, saying, What thing is this? what new doctrine is this? for with authority commandeth he even the unclean spirits, and they do obey him.

And immediately his fame spread abroad throughout all the region round about Galilee.

Luke 4, 31 - 37

And came down to Capernaum, a city of Galilee, and taught them on the sabbath days. And they were astonished at his doctrine; for his word was with power.

And in the synagogue there was a man, which had a spirit of an unclean devil, and cried out with a loud voice, saying, Let us alone; what have we to do with thee, thou Jesus of Nazareth? art thou come to destroy us? I know thee who thou art; the Holy One of God.

And Jesus rebuked him, saying, Hold thy peace, and come out of him. And when the devil had thrown him in the midst, he came out of him, and hurt him not.

And they were all amazed, and spake among themselves, saying, What a word is this! for with authority and power he commandeth the unclean spirits, and they come out.

37 And the fame of him went out into every place of the country round about.

Healing of the Mother in Law of Peter and other sick People

Matthew 8, 14 - 17

And when Jesus was come into Peter's house, he saw his wife's mother laid, and sick of a fever. And he touched her hand, and the fever left her; and she arose, and ministered unto them.

When the even was come, they brought unto him many that were possessed with devils; and he cast out the spirits with his word, and healed all that were sick;

That it might be fulfilled which was spoken by Esaias the prophet, saying, Himself took our infirmities, and bare our sicknesses.

Mark 1, 29 - 34

And forthwith, when they were come out of the synagogue, they entered into the house of Simon and Andrew, with James and John. But Simon's wife's mother lay sick of a fever, and anon they tell him of her.

And he came and took her by the hand, and lifted her up; and immediately the fever left her, and she ministered unto them. And at even, when the sun did set, they brought unto him all that were diseased, and them that were possessed with devils. And all the city was gathered together at the door.

And he healed many that were sick of divers diseases, and cast out many devils; and suffered not the devils to speak, because they knew him.

Luke 4, 38 - 41

And he arose out of the synagogue, and entered into Simon's house. And Simon's wife's mother was taken with a great fever; and they besought him for her. And he stood over her, and rebuked the fever; and it left her; and immediately she arose and ministered unto them.

Now when the sun was setting, all they that had any sick with divers diseases brought them unto him; and he laid his hands on every one of them, and healed them.

And devils also came out of many, crying out, and saying, Thou art Christ the Son of God. And he rebuking them suffered them not to speak; for they knew that he was Christ.

Disease Healing in Galilee

Matthew 4, 23 - 25

And Jesus went about all Galilee, teaching in their synagogues, and preaching the gospel of the kingdom, and healing all manner of sickness and all manner of disease among the people.

And his fame went throughout all Syria; and they brought unto him all sick people that were taken with divers diseases and torments, and those which were possessed with devils, and those which were lunatick, and those that had the palsy; and he healed them.

And there followed him great multitudes of people from Galilee, and from Decapolis, and from Jerusalem, and from Judaea, and from beyond Jordan.

Healing of a Leper

Matthew 8, 1 - 4

When he was come down from the mountain, great multitudes followed him. And, behold, there came a leper and worshipped him, saying, Lord, if thou wilt, thou canst make me clean.

And Jesus put forth his hand, and touched him, saying, I will; be thou clean.

And immediately his leprosy was cleansed.

And Jesus saith unto him, See thou tell no man; but go thy way, shew thyself to the priest, and offer the gift that Moses commanded, for a testimony unto them.

Mark 1, 40 - 44

And there came a leper to him, beseeching him, and kneeling down to him, and saying unto him, If thou wilt, thou canst make me clean.

And Jesus, moved with compassion, put forth his hand, and touched him, and saith unto him, I will; be thou clean.

And as soon as he had spoken, immediately the leprosy departed from him, and he was cleansed. And he straitly charged him, and forthwith sent him away; and saith unto him, See thou say nothing to any man; but go thy way, shew thyself to the priest, and offer for thy cleansing those things which Moses commanded, for a testimony unto them.

Luke 5, 12 - 14

And it came to pass, when he was in a certain city, behold a man full of leprosy; who seeing Jesus fell on his face, and besought him, saying, Lord, if thou wilt, thou canst make me clean.

And he put forth his hand, and touched him, saying, I will; be thou clean. And immediately the leprosy departed from him. And he charged him to tell no man; but go, and shew thyself to the priest, and offer for thy cleansing, according as Moses commanded, for a testimony unto them.

Healing of a Servant from the Centurion of Capernaum

Matthew 8, 5 - 13

And when Jesus was entered into Capernaum, there came unto him a centurion, beseeching him, and saying, Lord, my servant lieth at home sick of the palsy, grievously tormented.

And Jesus saith unto him, I will come and heal him.

The centurion answered and said, Lord, I am not worthy that thou shouldest come under my roof; but speak the word only, and my servant shall be healed. For I am a man under authority, having soldiers under me; and I say to this man, Go, and he goeth; and to another, Come, and he cometh; and to my servant, Do this, and he doeth it.

When Jesus heard it, he marvelled, and said to them that followed, Verily I say unto you, I have not found so great faith, no, not in Israel. And I say unto you, That many shall come from the east and west, and shall sit down with Abraham, and Isaac, and Jacob, in the kingdom of heaven. But the children of the kingdom shall be cast out into outer darkness; there shall be weeping and gnashing of teeth.

And Jesus said unto the centurion, Go thy way; and as thou hast believed, so be it done unto thee. And his servant was healed in the selfsame hour.

Luke 7, 1 - 10

Now when he had ended all his sayings in the audience of the people, he entered into Capernaum. And a certain centurion's servant, who was dear unto him, was sick, and ready to die. And when he heard of Jesus, he sent unto him the elders of the Jews, beseeching him that he would come and heal his servant.

And when they came to Jesus, they besought him instantly, saying, That he was worthy for whom he should do this; For he loveth our nation, and he hath built us a synagogue.

Then Jesus went with them. And when he was now not far from the house, the centurion sent friends to him, saying unto him, Lord, trouble not thyself; for I am not worthy that thou shouldest enter under my roof; Wherefore neither thought I myself worthy to come unto thee; but say in a word, and my servant shall be healed. For I also am a man set under authority, having under me soldiers, and I say unto one, Go, and he goeth; and to another, Come, and he cometh; and to my servant, Do this, and he doeth it.

When Jesus heard these things, he marvelled at him, and turned him about, and said unto the people that followed him, I say unto you, I have not found so great faith, no, not in Israel.

And they that were sent, returning to the house, found the servant whole that had been sick.

Healing of two Possessed in the Country of the Gergesenes

Matthew 8, 28 - 34

And when he was come to the other side into the country of the Gergesenes, there met him two possessed with devils, coming out of the tombs, exceeding fierce, so that no man might pass by that way.

And, behold, they cried out, saying, What have we to do with thee, Jesus, thou Son of God? art thou come hither to torment us before the time?

And there was a good way off from them an herd of many swine feeding. So the devils besought him, saying, If thou cast us out, suffer us to go away into the herd of swine.

And he said unto them, Go.

And when they were come out, they went into the herd of swine; and, behold, the whole herd of swine ran violently down a steep place into the sea, and perished in the waters. And they that kept them fled, and went their ways into the city, and told every thing, and what was befallen to the possessed of the devils.

And, behold, the whole city came out to meet Jesus; and when they saw him, they besought him that he would depart out of their coasts.

Luke 8, 26 - 39

And they arrived at the country of the Gadarenes, which is over against Galilee. And when he went forth to land, there met him out of the city a certain man, which had devils long time, and ware no clothes, neither abode in any house, but in the tombs.

When he saw Jesus, he cried out, and fell down before him, and with a loud voice said, What have I to do with thee, Jesus, thou Son of God most high? I beseech thee, torment me not.

(For he had commanded the unclean spirit to come out of the man. For oftentimes it had caught him; and he was kept bound with chains and in fetters; and he brake the bands, and was driven of the devil into the wilderness.)

And Jesus asked him, saying, What is thy name?

And he said, Legion; because many devils were entered into him.

And they besought him that he would not command them to go out into the deep.

And there was there an herd of many swine feeding on the mountain; and they besought him that he would suffer them to enter into them. And he suffered them.

Then went the devils out of the man, and entered into the swine; and the herd ran violently down a steep place into the lake, and were choked.

When they that fed them saw what was done, they fled, and went and told it in the city and in the country.

Then they went out to see what was done; and came to Jesus, and found the man, out of whom the devils were departed, sitting at the feet of Jesus, clothed, and in his right mind; and they were afraid.

They also which saw it told them by what means he that was possessed of the devils was healed.

Then the whole multitude of the country of the Gadarenes round about besought him to depart from them; for they were taken with great fear; and he went up into the ship, and returned back again.

Now the man out of whom the devils were departed besought him that he might be with him; but Jesus sent him away, saying,

Return to thine own house, and shew how great things God hath done unto thee. And he went his way, and published throughout the whole city how great things Jesus had done unto him.

Healing of a Sick of the Palsy

Matthew 9, 1 - 8

And he entered into a ship, and passed over, and came into his own city. And, behold, they brought to him a man sick of the palsy, lying on a bed; and Jesus seeing their faith said unto the sick of the palsy; Son, be of good cheer; thy sins be forgiven thee.

And, behold, certain of the scribes said within themselves, This man blasphemeth.

And Jesus knowing their thoughts said, Wherefore think ye evil in your hearts? For whether is easier, to say, Thy sins be forgiven thee; or to say, Arise, and walk? But that ye may know that the Son of man hath power on earth to forgive sins, (then saith he to the sick of the palsy,) Arise, take up thy bed, and go unto thine house.

And he arose, and departed to his house.

But when the multitudes saw it, they marvelled, and glorified God, which had given such power unto men.

Mark 2, 1 - 12

And again he entered into Capernaum after some days; and it was noised that he was in the house. And straightway many were gathered together, insomuch that there was no room to receive them, no, not so much as about the door; and he preached the word unto them.

And they come unto him, bringing one sick of the palsy, which was borne of four. And when they could not come nigh unto him for the press, they uncovered the roof where he was; and when they had broken it up, they let down the bed wherein the sick of the palsy lay.

When Jesus saw their faith, he said unto the sick of the palsy, Son, thy sins be forgiven thee.

But there was certain of the scribes sitting there, and reasoning in their hearts,

Why doth this man thus speak blasphemies? who can forgive sins but God only?

And immediately when Jesus perceived in his spirit that they so reasoned within themselves, he said unto them, Why reason ye these things in your hearts? Whether is it easier to say to the sick of the palsy, Thy sins be forgiven thee; or to say, Arise, and take up thy bed, and walk? But that ye may know that the Son of man hath power on earth to forgive sins, (he saith to the sick of the palsy,) I say unto thee, Arise, and take up thy bed, and go thy way into thine house.

And immediately he arose, took up the bed, and went forth before them all; insomuch that they were all amazed, and glorified God, saying, We never saw it on this fashion.

Luke 5, 17 - 26

And it came to pass on a certain day, as he was teaching, that there were Pharisees and doctors of the law sitting by, which were come out of every town of Galilee, and Judaea, and Jerusalem; and the power of the Lord was present to heal them. And, behold, men brought in a bed a man which was taken with a palsy; and they sought means to bring him in, and to lay him before him.

And when they could not find by what way they might bring him in because of the multitude, they went upon the housetop, and let him down through the tiling with his couch into the midst before Jesus.

And when he saw their faith, he said unto him, Man, thy sins are forgiven thee.

And the scribes and the Pharisees began to reason, saying, Who is this which speaketh blasphemies? Who can forgive sins, but God alone?

But when Jesus perceived their thoughts, he answering said unto them, What reason ye in your hearts? Whether is easier, to say, Thy sins be forgiven thee; or to say, Rise up and walk? But that ye may know that the Son of man hath power upon earth to forgive sins, (he said unto the sick of the palsy,) I say unto thee, Arise, and take up thy couch, and go into thine house.

And immediately he rose up before them, and took up that whereon he lay, and departed to his own house, glorifying God.

And they were all amazed, and they glorified God, and were filled with fear, saying, We have seen strange things to day.

Healing of the Issued with Blood and the Raising of Jairus' Daughter

Matthew 9, 18 - 26

While he spake these things unto them, behold, there came a certain ruler, and worshipped him, saying, My daughter is even now dead; but come and lay thy hand upon her, and she shall live.

And Jesus arose, and followed him, and so did his disciples. And, behold, a woman, which was diseased with an issue of blood twelve years, came behind him, and touched the hem of his garment; For she said within herself, If I may but touch his garment, I shall be whole.

But Jesus turned him about, and when he saw her, he said, Daughter, be of good comfort; thy faith hath made thee whole.

And the woman was made whole from that hour.

And when Jesus came into the ruler's house, and saw the minstrels and the people making a noise, he said unto them, Give place; for the maid is not dead, but sleepeth. And they laughed him to scorn.

But when the people were put forth, he went in, and took her by the hand, and the maid arose. And the fame hereof went abroad into all that land.

Mark 5, 21 - 43

And when Jesus was passed over again by ship unto the other side, much people gathered unto him; and he was nigh unto the sea. And, behold, there cometh one of the rulers of the synagogue, Jairus by name; and when he saw him, he fell at his feet, and besought him greatly, saying, My little daughter lieth at the point of death; I pray thee, come and lay thy hands on her, that she may be healed; and she shall live.

And Jesus went with him; and much people followed him, and thronged him. And a certain woman, which had an issue of blood twelve years, and had suffered many things of many physicians, and had spent all that she had, and was nothing bettered, but rather grew worse, when she had heard of Jesus, came in the press behind, and touched his garment. For she said, If I may touch but his clothes, I shall be whole.

And straightway the fountain of her blood was dried up; and she felt in her body that she was healed of that plague.

And Jesus, immediately knowing in himself that virtue had gone out of him, turned him about in the press, and said, Who touched my clothes?

And his disciples said unto him, Thou seest the multitude thronging thee, and sayest thou, Who touched me?

And he looked round about to see her that had done this thing. But the woman fearing and trembling, knowing what was done in her, came and fell down before him, and told him all the truth. And he said unto her, Daughter, thy faith hath made thee whole; go in peace, and be whole of thy plague.

While he yet spake, there came from the ruler of the synagogue's house certain which said, Thy daughter is dead; why troublest thou the Master any further?

As soon as Jesus heard the word that was spoken, he saith unto the ruler of the synagogue, Be not afraid, only believe.

And he suffered no man to follow him, save Peter, and James, and John the brother of James. And he cometh to the house of the ruler of the synagogue, and seeth the tumult, and them that wept and wailed greatly. And when he was come in, he saith unto them, Why make ye this ado, and weep? the damsel is not dead, but sleepeth.

And they laughed him to scorn. But when he had put them all out, he taketh the father and the mother of the damsel, and them that were with him, and entereth in where the damsel was lying. And he took the damsel by the hand, and said unto her, Talitha cumi; which is, being interpreted, Damsel, I say unto thee, arise.

And straightway the damsel arose, and walked; for she was of the age of twelve years. And they were astonished with a great astonishment.

And he charged them straitly that no man should know it; and commanded that something should be given her to eat.

Luke 8, 40 - 56

And it came to pass, that, when Jesus was returned, the people gladly received him; for they were all waiting for him. And, behold, there came a man named Jairus, and he was a ruler of the synagogue; and he fell down at Jesus' feet, and besought him that he would come into his house; For he had one only daughter, about twelve years of age, and she lay a dying. But as he went the people thronged him.

And a woman having an issue of blood twelve years, which had spent all her living upon physicians, neither could be healed of any, came behind him, and touched the border of his garment; and immediately her issue of blood stanched. And Jesus said, Who touched me?

When all denied, Peter and they that were with him said, Master, the multitude throng thee and press thee, and sayest thou, Who touched me?

And Jesus said, Somebody hath touched me; for I perceive that virtue is gone out of me.

And when the woman saw that she was not hid, she came trembling, and falling down before him, she declared unto him before all the people for what cause she had touched him, and how she was healed immediately.

And he said unto her, Daughter, be of good comfort; thy faith hath made thee whole; go in peace.

While he yet spake, there cometh one from the ruler of the synagogue's house, saying to him, Thy daughter is dead; trouble not the Master.

But when Jesus heard it, he answered him, saying, Fear not; believe only, and she shall be made whole.

And when he came into the house, he suffered no man to go in, save Peter, and James, and John, and the father and the mother of the maiden. And all wept, and bewailed her; but he said, Weep not; she is not dead, but sleepeth.

And they laughed him to scorn, knowing that she was dead. And he put them all out, and took her by the hand, and called, saying, Maid, arise.

And her spirit came again, and she arose straightway; and he commanded to give her meat. And her parents were astonished; but he charged them that they should tell no man what was done.

Healing of two Blinds

Matthew 9, 27 - 31

And when Jesus departed thence, two blind men followed him, crying, and saying, Thou son of David, have mercy on us.

And when he was come into the house, the blind men came to him; and Jesus saith unto them, Believe ye that I am able to do this?

They said unto him, Yea, Lord.

Then touched he their eyes, saying, According to your faith be it unto you.

And their eyes were opened; and Jesus straitly charged them, saying, See that no man know it.

But they, when they were departed, spread abroad his fame in all that country.

Healing a dumb Man

Matthew 9, 32 - 34

As they went out, behold, they brought to him a dumb man possessed with a devil. And when the devil was cast out, the dumb spake; and the multitudes marvelled, saying, It was never so seen in Israel.

But the Pharisees said, He casteth out devils through the prince of the devils.

Luke 11, 14 - 16

And he was casting out a devil, and it was dumb. And it came to pass, when the devil was gone out, the dumb spake; and the people wondered.

But some of them said, He casteth out devils through Beelzebub the chief of the devils. And others, tempting him, sought of him a sign from heaven.

Healing a Man with a withered Hand on the Sabbath

Matthew 12, 9 - 14

And when he was departed thence, he went into their synagogue; And, behold, there was a man which had his hand withered. And they asked him, saying, Is it lawful to heal on the sabbath days? that they might accuse him.

And he said unto them, What man shall there be among you, that shall have one sheep, and if it fall into a pit on the sabbath day, will he not lay hold on it, and lift it out? How much then is a man better than a sheep? Wherefore it is lawful to do well on the sabbath days.

Then saith he to the man, Stretch forth thine hand.

And he stretched it forth; and it was restored whole, like as the other.

Then the Pharisees went out, and held a council against him, how they might destroy him.

Mark 3, 1 - 6

And he entered again into the synagogue; and there was a man there which had a withered hand. And they watched him, whether he would heal him on the sabbath day; that they might accuse him. And he saith unto the man which had the withered hand, Stand forth.

And he saith unto them, Is it lawful to do good on the sabbath days, or to do evil? to save life, or to kill?

But they held their peace.

And when he had looked round about on them with anger, being grieved for the hardness of their hearts, he saith unto the man, Stretch forth thine hand.

And he stretched it out; and his hand was restored whole as the other.

And the Pharisees went forth, and straightway took counsel with the Herodians against him, how they might destroy him.

Luke 6, 6 - 11

And it came to pass also on another sabbath, that he entered into the synagogue and taught; and there was a man whose right hand was withered. And the scribes and Pharisees watched him, whether he would heal on the sabbath day; that they might find an accusation against him.

But he knew their thoughts, and said to the man which had the withered hand, Rise up, and stand forth in the midst.

And he arose and stood forth.

Then said Jesus unto them, I will ask you one thing; Is it lawful on the sabbath days to do good, or to do evil? to save life, or to destroy it?

And looking round about upon them all, he said unto the man, Stretch forth thy hand.

And he did so; and his hand was restored whole as the other.

And they were filled with madness; and communed one with another what they might do to Jesus.

Raising of the Youth of Nain

Luke 7, 11 - 17

And it came to pass the day after, that he went into a city called Nain; and many of his disciples went with him, and much people. Now when he came nigh to the gate of the city, behold, there was a dead man carried out, the only son of his mother, and she was a widow; and much people of the city was with her.

And when the Lord saw her, he had compassion on her, and said unto her, Weep not.

And he came and touched the bier; and they that bare him stood still. And he said, Young man, I say unto thee, Arise.

And he that was dead sat up, and began to speak. And he delivered him to his mother.

And there came a fear on all; and they glorified God, saying, That a great prophet is risen up among us; and, That God hath visited his people. And this rumour of him went forth throughout all Judaea, and throughout all the region round about.

Healing at the See Gennesaret

Matthew 14, 34 - 36

And when they were gone over, they came into the land of Gennesaret.

And when the men of that place had knowledge of him, they sent out into all that country round about, and brought unto him all that were diseased; And besought him that they might only touch the hem of his garment; and as many as touched were made perfectly whole.

Mark 6, 53 - 56

And when they had passed over, they came into the land of Gennesaret, and drew to the shore. And when they were come out of the ship, straightway they knew him, And ran through that whole region round about, and began to carry about in beds those that were sick, where they heard he was.

And whithersoever he entered, into villages, or cities, or country, they laid the sick in the streets, and besought him that they might touch if it were but the border of his garment; and as many as touched him were made whole.

Distant Healing of the Daughter of a Woman from Canaan

Matthew 15, 21 – 28

Then Jesus went thence, and departed into the coasts of Tyre and Sidon. And, behold, a woman of Canaan came out of the same coasts, and cried unto him, saying, Have mercy on me, O Lord, thou son of David; my daughter is grievously vexed with a devil.

But he answered her not a word. And his disciples came and besought him, saying, Send her away; for she crieth after us.

But he answered and said, I am not sent but unto the lost sheep of the house of Israel.

Then came she and worshipped him, saying, Lord, help me.

But he answered and said, It is not meet to take the children's bread, and to cast it to dogs.

And she said, Truth, Lord; yet the dogs eat of the crumbs which fall from their masters' table.

Then Jesus answered and said unto her, O woman, great is thy faith; be it unto thee even as thou wilt.

And her daughter was made whole from that very hour.

Mark 7, 24 – 30

And from thence he arose, and went into the borders of Tyre and Sidon, and entered into an house, and would have no man know it; but he could not be hid. For a certain woman, whose young daughter had an unclean spirit, heard of him, and came and fell at his feet;

The woman was a Greek, a Syrophenician by nation; and she besought him that he would cast forth the devil out of her daughter.

But Jesus said unto her, Let the children first be filled; for it is not meet to take the children's bread, and to cast it unto the dogs.

And she answered and said unto him, Yes, Lord; yet the dogs under the table eat of the children's crumbs.

And he said unto her, For this saying go thy way; the devil is gone out of thy daughter.

And when she was come to her house, she found the devil gone out, and her daughter laid upon the bed.

Further Healings at the Galilee Sea

Matthew 15, 29 – 31

And Jesus departed from thence, and came nigh unto the sea of Galilee; and went up into a mountain, and sat down there. And great multitudes came unto him, having with them those that were lame, blind, dumb, maimed, and many others, and cast them down at Jesus' feet; and he healed them;

Insomuch that the multitude wondered, when they saw the dumb to speak, the maimed to be whole, the lame to walk, and the blind to see; and they glorified the God of Israel.

Mark 7, 31 – 37

And again, departing from the coasts of Tyre and Sidon, he came unto the sea of Galilee, through the midst of the coasts of Decapolis. And they bring unto him one that was deaf, and had an impediment in his speech; and they beseech him to put his hand upon him.

And he took him aside from the multitude, and put his fingers into his ears, and he spit, and touched his tongue; And looking up to heaven, he sighed, and saith unto him, Ephphatha, that is, Be opened.

And straightway his ears were opened, and the string of his tongue was loosed, and he spake plain.

And he charged them that they should tell no man; but the more he charged them, so much the more a great deal they published it;

And were beyond measure astonished, saying, He hath done all things well; he maketh both the deaf to hear, and the dumb to speak.

Healing of an epileptic Boy

Matthew 17, 14 – 21

And when they were come to the multitude, there came to him a certain man, kneeling down to him, and saying, Lord, have mercy on my son; for he is lunatick, and sore vexed; for ofttimes he falleth into the fire, and oft into the water. And I brought him to thy disciples, and they could not cure him.

Then Jesus answered and said, O faithless and perverse generation, how long shall I be with you? how long shall I suffer you? bring him hither to me.

And Jesus rebuked the devil; and he departed out of him; and the child was cured from that very hour.

Then came the disciples to Jesus apart, and said, Why could not we cast him out?

And Jesus said unto them, Because of your unbelief; for verily I say unto you, If ye have faith as a grain of mustard seed, ye shall say unto this mountain, Remove hence to yonder place; and it shall remove; and nothing shall be impossible unto you. Howbeit this kind goeth not out but by prayer and fasting.

Mark 9, 14 – 29

And when he came to his disciples, he saw a great multitude about them, and the scribes questioning with them. And straightway all the people, when they beheld him, were greatly amazed, and running to him saluted him. And he asked the scribes, What question ye with them?

And one of the multitude answered and said, Master, I have brought unto thee my son, which hath a dumb spirit; And wheresoever he taketh him, he teareth him; and he foameth, and gnasheth with his teeth, and pineth away; and I spake to thy disciples that they should cast him out; and they could not.

He answereth him, and saith, O faithless generation, how long shall I be with you? how long shall I suffer you? bring him unto me.

And they brought him unto him; and when he saw him, straightway the spirit tare him; and he fell on the ground, and wallowed foaming.

And he asked his father, How long is it ago since this came unto him?

And he said, Of a child. And ofttimes it hath cast him into the fire, and into the waters, to destroy him; but if thou canst do any thing, have compassion on us, and help us.

Jesus said unto him, If thou canst believe, all things are possible to him that believeth.

And straightway the father of the child cried out, and said with tears, Lord, I believe; help thou mine unbelief.

When Jesus saw that the people came running together, he rebuked the foul spirit, saying unto him, Thou dumb and deaf spirit, I charge thee, come out of him, and enter no more into him.

And the spirit cried, and rent him sore, and came out of him; and he was as one dead; insomuch that many said, He is dead.

But Jesus took him by the hand, and lifted him up; and he arose. And when he was come into the house, his disciples asked him privately, Why could not we cast him out?

And he said unto them, This kind can come forth by nothing, but by prayer and fasting.

Luke 9, 38 – 42

And, behold, a man of the company cried out, saying, Master, I beseech thee, look upon my son; for he is mine only child. And, lo, a spirit taketh him, and he suddenly crieth out; and it teareth him that he foameth again, and bruising him hardly departeth from him.

And I besought thy disciples to cast him out; and they could not.

And Jesus answering said, O faithless and perverse generation, how long shall I be with you, and suffer you? Bring thy son hither.

And as he was yet a coming, the devil threw him down, and tare him. And Jesus rebuked the unclean spirit, and healed the child, and delivered him again to his father.

Healing of a blind and dumb Man

Matthew 12, 22

Then was brought unto him one possessed with a devil, blind, and dumb; and he healed him, insomuch that the blind and dumb both spake and saw.

Healing
of a crooked Woman on a Sabbath

Luke 13, 10 – 17

And he was teaching in one of the synagogues on the sabbath. And, behold, there was a woman which had a spirit of infirmity eighteen years, and was bowed together, and could in no wise lift up herself. And when Jesus saw her, he called her to him, and said unto her, Woman, thou art loosed from thine infirmity.

And he laid his hands on her; and immediately she was made straight, and glorified God.

And the ruler of the synagogue answered with indignation, because that Jesus had healed on the sabbath day, and said unto the people, There are six days in which men ought to work; in them therefore come and be healed, and not on the sabbath day.

The Lord then answered him, and said, Thou hypocrite, doth not each one of you on the sabbath loose his ox or his ass from the stall, and lead him away to watering?

And ought not this woman, being a daughter of Abraham, whom Satan hath bound, lo, these eighteen years, be loosed from this bond on the sabbath day?

And when he had said these things, all his adversaries were ashamed; and all the people rejoiced for all the glorious things that were done by him.

Healing of a Blind in Bethsaida

Mark 8, 22 – 26

And he cometh to Bethsaida; and they bring a blind man unto him, and besought him to touch him.

And he took the blind man by the hand, and led him out of the town; and when he had spit on his eyes, and put his hands upon him, he asked him if he saw ought.

And he looked up, and said, I see men as trees, walking.

After that he put his hands again upon his eyes, and made him look up; and he was restored, and saw every man clearly.

And he sent him away to his house, saying, Neither go into the town, nor tell it to any in the town.

Healing a Dropsy on the Sabbath

Luke 14, 1 - 6

And it came to pass, as he went into the house of one of the chief Pharisees to eat bread on the sabbath day, that they watched him. And, behold, there was a certain man before him which had the dropsy.

And Jesus answering spake unto the lawyers and Pharisees, saying, Is it lawful to heal on the sabbath day?

And they held their peace. And he took him, and healed him, and let him go;

And answered them, saying, Which of you shall have an ass or an ox fallen into a pit, and will not straightway pull him out on the sabbath day?

And they could not answer him again to these things.

Healing of the ten Lepers

Luke 17, 11 – 19

And it came to pass, as he went to Jerusalem, that he passed through the midst of Samaria and Galilee. And as he entered into a certain village, there met him ten men that were lepers, which stood afar off; And they lifted up their voices, and said, Jesus, Master, have mercy on us.

And when he saw them, he said unto them, Go shew yourselves unto the priests.

And it came to pass, that, as they went, they were cleansed.

And one of them, when he saw that he was healed, turned back, and with a loud voice glorified God, and fell down on his face at his feet, giving him thanks; and he was a Samaritan.

And Jesus answering said, Were there not ten cleansed? but where are the nine? There are not found that returned to give glory to God, save this stranger.

And he said unto him, Arise, go thy way; thy faith hath made thee whole.

Healing of a Blind at Jericho

Matthew 20, 29 – 34

And as they departed from Jericho, a great multitude followed him. And, behold, two blind men sitting by the way side, when they heard that Jesus passed by, cried out, saying, Have mercy on us, O Lord, thou son of David.

And the multitude rebuked them, because they should hold their peace; but they cried the more, saying, Have mercy on us, O Lord, thou son of David.

And Jesus stood still, and called them, and said, What will ye that I shall do unto you?

They say unto him, Lord, that our eyes may be opened.

So Jesus had compassion on them, and touched their eyes; and immediately their eyes received sight, and they followed him.

Mark 10, 46 – 52

And they came to Jericho; and as he went out of Jericho with his disciples and a great number of people, blind Bartimaeus, the son of Timaeus, sat by the highway side begging.

And when he heard that it was Jesus of Nazareth, he began to cry out, and say, Jesus, thou son of David, have mercy on me.

And many charged him that he should hold his peace; but he cried the more a great deal, Thou son of David, have mercy on me.

And Jesus stood still, and commanded him to be called. And they call the blind man, saying unto him, Be of good comfort, rise; he calleth thee.

And he, casting away his garment, rose, and came to Jesus. And Jesus answered and said unto him, What wilt thou that I should do unto thee?

The blind man said unto him, Lord, that I might receive my sight.

And Jesus said unto him, Go thy way; thy faith hath made thee whole.

And immediately he received his sight, and followed Jesus in the way.

Luke 18, 35 – 43

And it came to pass, that as he was come nigh unto Jericho, a certain blind man sat by the way side begging; And hearing the multitude pass by, he asked what it meant.

And they told him, that Jesus of Nazareth passeth by.

And he cried, saying, Jesus, thou son of David, have mercy on me.

And they which went before rebuked him, that he should hold his peace; but he cried so much the more, Thou son of David, have mercy on me.

And Jesus stood, and commanded him to be brought unto him; and when he was come near, he asked him, saying, What wilt thou that I shall do unto thee?

And he said, Lord, that I may receive my sight.

And Jesus said unto him, Receive thy sight; thy faith hath saved thee.

And immediately he received his sight, and followed him, glorifying God; and all the people, when they saw it, gave praise unto God.

Healing of the Son of a royal Official in Capernaum

John 4, 46 – 53

So Jesus came again into Cana of Galilee, where he made the water wine. And there was a certain nobleman, whose son was sick at Capernaum. When he heard that Jesus was come out of Judaea into Galilee, he went unto him, and besought him that he would come down, and heal his son; for he was at the point of death. Then said Jesus unto him, Except ye see signs and wonders, ye will not believe.

The nobleman saith unto him, Sir, come down ere my child die.

Jesus saith unto him, Go thy way; thy son liveth.

And the man believed the word that Jesus had spoken unto him, and he went his way. And as he was now going down, his servants met him, and told him, saying, Thy son liveth.

Then enquired he of them the hour when he began to amend. And they said unto him, Yesterday at the seventh hour the fever left him.

So the father knew that it was at the same hour, in the which Jesus said unto him, Thy son liveth; and himself believed, and his whole house.

Healing of the Paralyzed in Bethesda

John 5, 1 – 18

After this there was a feast of the Jews; and Jesus went up to Jerusalem. Now there is at Jerusalem by the sheep market a pool, which is called in the Hebrew tongue Bethesda, having five porches. In these lay a great multitude of impotent folk, of blind, halt, withered, waiting for the moving of the water. For an angel went down at a certain season into the pool, and troubled the water; whosoever then first after the troubling of the water stepped in was made whole of whatsoever disease he had.

And a certain man was there, which had an infirmity thirty and eight years. When Jesus saw him lie, and knew that he had been now a long time in that case, he saith unto him, Wilt thou be made whole?

The impotent man answered him, Sir, I have no man, when the water is troubled, to put me into the pool; but while I am coming, another steppeth down before me.

Jesus saith unto him, Rise, take up thy bed, and walk.

And immediately the man was made whole, and took up his bed, and walked;

And on the same day was the sabbath. The Jews therefore said unto him that was cured, It is the sabbath day; it is not lawful for thee to carry thy bed.

He answered them, He that made me whole, the same said unto me, Take up thy bed, and walk.

Then asked they him, What man is that which said unto thee, Take up thy bed, and walk?

And he that was healed wist not who it was; for Jesus had conveyed himself away, a multitude being in that place.

Afterward Jesus findeth him in the temple, and said unto him, Behold, thou art made whole; sin no more, lest a worse thing come unto thee.

The man departed, and told the Jews that it was Jesus, which had made him whole. And therefore did the Jews persecute Jesus, and sought to slay him, because he had done these things on the sabbath day. But Jesus answered them, My Father worketh hitherto, and I work.

Therefore the Jews sought the more to kill him, because he not only had broken the sabbath, but said also that God was his Father, making himself equal with God.

Healing of a Blind by Birth at the Pool of Siloam

John 9, 1 – 7

And as Jesus passed by, he saw a man which was blind from his birth. And his disciples asked him, saying, Master, who did sin, this man, or his parents, that he was born blind?

Jesus answered, Neither hath this man sinned, nor his parents; but that the works of God should be made manifest in him. I must work the works of him that sent me, while it is day; the night cometh, when no man can work. As long as I am in the world, I am the light of the world.

When he had thus spoken, he spat on the ground, and made clay of the spittle, and he anointed the eyes of the blind man with the clay, and said unto him, Go, wash in the pool of Siloam, (which is by interpretation, Sent.) He went his way therefore, and washed, and came seeing.

Raising Lazarus from the Dead

John 11, 1 - 44

Now a certain man was sick, named Lazarus, of Bethany, the town of Mary and her sister Martha. (It was that Mary which anointed the Lord with ointment, and wiped his feet with her hair, whose brother Lazarus was sick.) Therefore his sisters sent unto him, saying, Lord, behold, he whom thou lovest is sick.

When Jesus heard that, he said, This sickness is not unto death, but for the glory of God, that the Son of God might be glorified thereby.

Now Jesus loved Martha, and her sister, and Lazarus. When he had heard therefore that he was sick, he abode two days still in the same place where he was. Then after that saith he to his disciples, Let us go into Judaea again.

His disciples say unto him, Master, the Jews of late sought to stone thee; and goest thou thither again?

Jesus answered, Are there not twelve hours in the day? If any man walk in the day, he stumbleth not, because he seeth the light of this world. But if a man walk in the night, he stumbleth, because there is no light in him.

These things said he; and after that he saith unto them, Our friend Lazarus sleepeth; but I go, that I may awake him out of sleep.

Then said his disciples, Lord, if he sleep, he shall do well.

Howbeit Jesus spake of his death; but they thought that he had spoken of taking of rest in sleep. Then said Jesus unto them plainly, Lazarus is dead.

And I am glad for your sakes that I was not there, to the intent ye may believe; nevertheless let us go unto him.

Then said Thomas, which is called Didymus, unto his fellowdisciples, Let us also go, that we may die with him.

Then when Jesus came, he found that he had lain in the grave four days already.

Now Bethany was nigh unto Jerusalem, about fifteen furlongs off; And many of the Jews came to Martha and Mary, to comfort them concerning their brother. Then Martha, as soon as she heard that Jesus was coming, went and met him; but Mary sat still in the house. Then said Martha unto Jesus, Lord, if thou hadst been here, my brother had not died. But I know, that even now, whatsoever thou wilt ask of God, God will give it thee.

Jesus saith unto her, Thy brother shall rise again.

Martha saith unto him, I know that he shall rise again in the resurrection at the last day.

Jesus said unto her, I am the resurrection, and

the life; he that believeth in me, though he were dead, yet shall he live; and whosoever liveth and believeth in me shall never die. Believest thou this?

She saith unto him, Yea, Lord; I believe that thou art the Christ, the Son of God, which should come into the world.

And when she had so said, she went her way, and called Mary her sister secretly, saying, The Master is come, and calleth for thee. As soon as she heard that, she arose quickly, and came unto him. Now Jesus was not yet come into the town, but was in that place where Martha met him.

The Jews then which were with her in the house, and comforted her, when they saw Mary, that she rose up hastily and went out, followed her, saying, She goeth unto the grave to weep there. Then when Mary was come where Jesus was, and saw him, she fell down at his feet, saying unto him, Lord, if thou hadst been here, my brother had not died.

When Jesus therefore saw her weeping, and the Jews also weeping which came with her, he groaned in the spirit, and was troubled. And said, Where have ye laid him?

They said unto him, Lord, come and see.

Jesus wept.

Then said the Jews, Behold how he loved him!

And some of them said, Could not this man, which opened the eyes of the blind, have caused that even this man should not have died?

Jesus therefore again groaning in himself cometh to the grave. It was a cave, and a stone lay upon it. Jesus said, Take ye away the stone.

Martha, the sister of him that was dead, saith unto him, Lord, by this time he stinketh; for he hath been dead four days.

Jesus saith unto her, Said I not unto thee, that, if thou wouldest believe, thou shouldest see the glory of God?

Then they took away the stone from the place where the dead was laid. And Jesus lifted up his eyes, and said, Father, I thank thee that thou hast heard me. And I knew that thou hearest me always; but because of the people which stand by I said it, that they may believe that thou hast sent me.

And when he thus had spoken, he cried with a loud voice, Lazarus, come forth.

And he that was dead came forth, bound hand and foot with graveclothes; and his face was bound about with a napkin.

Jesus saith unto them, Loose him, and let him go.

The Command of Jesus to his Disciples

Our Mission in the World

Matthew 10, 1

And when he had called unto him his twelve disciples, he gave them power against unclean spirits, to cast them out, and to heal all manner of sickness and all manner of disease.

Matthew 10, 5 - 16

These twelve Jesus sent forth, and commanded them, saying, Go not into the way of the Gentiles, and into any city of the Samaritans enter ye not: But go rather to the lost sheep of the house of Israel. And as ye go, preach, saying, The kingdom of heaven is at hand. Heal the sick, cleanse the lepers, raise the dead, cast out devils: freely ye have received, freely give.

Provide neither gold, nor silver, nor brass in your purses, Nor scrip for your journey, neither two coats, neither shoes, nor yet staves: for the workman is worthy of his meat.

And into whatsoever city or town ye shall enter, enquire who in it is worthy; and there abide till ye go thence.

And when ye come into an house, salute it. And if the house be worthy, let your peace come upon it: but if it be not worthy, let your peace return to you. And whosoever shall not receive you, nor hear your words, when ye depart out of that house or city, shake off the dust of your feet.

Verily I say unto you, It shall be more tolerable for the land of Sodom and Gomorrha in the day of judgment, than for that city.

Behold, I send you forth as sheep in the midst of wolves: be ye therefore wise as serpents, and harmless as doves.

Luke 9, 1 - 6

Then he called his twelve disciples together, and gave them power and authority over all devils, and to cure diseases. And he sent them to preach the kingdom of God, and to heal the sick.

And he said unto them, Take nothing for your journey, neither staves, nor scrip, neither bread, neither money; neither have two coats apiece.

And whatsoever house ye enter into, there abide, and thence depart. And whosoever will not receive you, when ye go out of that city, shake off the very dust from your feet for a testimony against them.

And they departed, and went through the towns, preaching the gospel, and healing every where.

Luke 24, 49

And, behold,
I send the promise of my Father upon you.

Mark 16, 15 - 18

And he said unto them, Go ye into all the world, and preach the gospel to every creature. He that believeth and is baptized shall be saved; but he that believeth not shall be damned.

And these signs shall follow them that believe: In my name shall they cast out devils; they shall speak with new tongues; they shall take up serpents; and if they drink any deadly thing, it shall not hurt them; they shall lay hands on the sick, and they shall recover.

Matthew 28, 16 - 20

Then the eleven disciples went away into Galilee, into a mountain where Jesus had appointed them. And when they saw him, they worshipped him: but some doubted.

And Jesus came and spake unto them, saying, All power is given unto me in heaven and in earth. Go ye therefore, and teach all nations, baptizing them in the name of the Father, and of the Son, and of the Holy Ghost:

Teaching them to observe all things whatsoever I have commanded you: and, lo, I am with you always, even unto the end of the world.

Amen.

Mark 6, 12 - 13

And they went out, and preached that men should repent. And they cast out many devils, and anointed with oil many that were sick, and healed them.

Mark 16, 20

And they went forth, and preached every where, the Lord working with them, and confirming the word with signs following.

Amen.

Acts 1, 8

But ye shall receive power, after that the Holy Ghost is come upon you: and ye shall be witnesses unto me both in Jerusalem, and in all Judaea, and in Samaria, and unto the uttermost part of the earth.

1. Corinthians 6, 19

What? know ye not that your body is the temple of the Holy Ghost which is in you, which ye have of God, and ye are not your own?

Healing Miracles of the Apostles

Healing of a paralyzed Man through Peter

Acts 3, 1 – 16

Now Peter and John went up together into the temple at the hour of prayer, being the ninth hour. And a certain man lame from his mother's womb was carried, whom they laid daily at the gate of the temple which is called Beautiful, to ask alms of them that entered into the temple; who seeing Peter and John about to go into the temple asked an alms.

And Peter, fastening his eyes upon him with John, said, Look on us.

And he gave heed unto them, expecting to receive something of them.

Then Peter said, Silver and gold have I none; but such as I have give I thee: In the name of Jesus Christ of Nazareth rise up and walk.

And he took him by the right hand, and lifted him up: and immediately his feet and ankle bones received strength. And he leaping up stood, and walked, and entered with them into the temple, walking, and leaping, and praising God. And all the people saw him walking and praising God.

And they knew that it was he which sat for alms at the Beautiful gate of the temple: and they were filled with wonder and amazement at that which had happened unto him.

And as the lame man which was healed held Peter and John, all the people ran together unto them in the porch that is called Solomon's, greatly wondering. And when Peter saw it, he answered unto the people, Ye men of Israel, why marvel ye at this? or why look ye so earnestly on us, as though by our own power or holiness we had made this man to walk?

The God of Abraham, and of Isaac, and of Jacob, the God of our fathers, hath glorified his Son Jesus; whom ye delivered up, and denied him in the presence of Pilate, when he was determined to let him go. But ye denied the Holy One and the Just, and desired a murderer to be granted unto you; and killed the Prince of life, whom God hath raised from the dead; whereof we are witnesses.

And his name through faith in his name hath made this man strong, whom ye see and know: yea, the faith which is by him hath given him this perfect soundness in the presence of you all.

Indefinite Number of Healings through Peter in Jerusalem

Acts 5, 12 – 16

And by the hands of the apostles were many signs and wonders wrought among the people; (and they were all with one accord in Solomon's porch. And of the rest durst no man join himself to them: but the people magnified them.

And believers were the more added to the Lord, multitudes both of men and women.)

Insomuch that they brought forth the sick into the streets, and laid them on beds and couches, that at the least the shadow of Peter passing by might overshadow some of them.

There came also a multitude out of the cities round about unto Jerusalem, bringing sick folks, and them which were vexed with unclean spirits: and they were healed every one.

Healing of Demon-Possessed, Paralyzed and Crippled through Philip in Samaria

Acts 8, 6 - 8

And the people with one accord gave heed unto those things which Philip spake, hearing and seeing the miracles which he did.

For unclean spirits, crying with loud voice, came out of many that were possessed with them: and many taken with palsies, and that were lame, were healed. And there was great joy in that city.

Healing of the blind Saul

Acts 9, 17 – 18

And Ananias went his way, and entered into the house; and putting his hands on him said, Brother Saul, the Lord, even Jesus, that appeared unto thee in the way as thou camest, hath sent me, that thou mightest receive thy sight, and be filled with the Holy Ghost.

And immediately there fell from his eyes as it had been scales: and he received sight forthwith, and arose, and was baptized.

Raising Tabita from the Dead

Acts 9, 36 – 42

Now there was at Joppa a certain disciple named Tabitha, which by interpretation is called Dorcas: this woman was full of good works and almsdeeds which she did. And it came to pass in those days, that she was sick, and died: whom when they had washed, they laid her in an upper chamber. And forasmuch as Lydda was nigh to Joppa, and the disciples had heard that Peter was there, they sent unto him two men, desiring him that he would not delay to come to them.

Then Peter arose and went with them. When he was come, they brought him into the upper chamber; and all the widows stood by him weeping, and shewing the coats and garments which Dorcas made, while she was with them.

But Peter put them all forth, and kneeled down, and prayed; and turning him to the body said, Tabitha, arise.

And she opened her eyes: and when she saw Peter, she sat up.

And he gave her his hand, and lifted her up, and when he had called the saints and widows, presented her alive.

And it was known throughout all Joppa; and many believed in the Lord.

Healing of a Paralyzed in Lystra

Acts 14, 8 – 10

And there sat a certain man at Lystra, impotent in his feet, being a cripple from his mother's womb, who never had walked; The same heard Paul speak, who stedfastly beholding him, and perceiving that he had faith to be healed,

Said with a loud voice, Stand upright on thy feet. And he leaped and walked.

Healing of sick People in Ephesus

Acts 19, 11 - 12

And God wrought special miracles by the hands of Paul:

So that from his body were brought unto the sick handkerchiefs or aprons, and the diseases departed from them, and the evil spirits went out of them.

Eutychus is raised from the Dead by Paul

Acts 20, 7 – 12

And upon the first day of the week, when the disciples came together to break bread, Paul preached unto them, ready to depart on the morrow; and continued his speech until midnight. And there were many lights in the upper chamber, where they were gathered together.

And there sat in a window a certain young man named Eutychus, being fallen into a deep sleep: and as Paul was long preaching, he sunk down with sleep, and fell down from the third loft, and was taken up dead.

And Paul went down, and fell on him, and embracing him said, Trouble not yourselves; for his life is in him.

When he therefore was come up again, and had broken bread, and eaten, and talked a long while, even till break of day, so he departed. And they brought the young man alive, and were not a little comforted.

Healing of Publius' Father and other sick People in Malta

Acts 28, 8 – 9

And it came to pass, that the father of Publius lay sick of a fever and of a bloody flux, to whom Paul entered in, and prayed, and laid his hands on him, and healed him.

So when this was done, others also, which had diseases in the island, came, and were healed.

**Casting out Demons
in the Name of Jesus
by a non-disciple**

Luke 9, 49 – 50

And John answered and said, Master, we saw one casting out devils in thy name; and we forbad him, because he followeth not with us.

And Jesus said unto him, Forbid him not: for he that is not against us is for us.

Mark 9, 38 – 41

And John answered him, saying, Master, we saw one casting out devils in thy name, and he followeth not us: and we forbad him, because he followeth not us.

But Jesus said, Forbid him not: for there is no man which shall do a miracle in my name, that can lightly speak evil of me. For he that is not against us is on our part. For whosoever shall give you a cup of water to drink in my name, because ye belong to Christ, verily I say unto you, he shall not lose his reward.

*The Power of God,
working through Jesus*

John 5, 19

Then answered Jesus and said unto them, Verily, verily, I say unto you, The Son can do nothing of himself, but what he seeth the Father do: for what things soever he doeth, these also doeth the Son likewise.

John 8, 28

Then said Jesus unto them, When ye have lifted up the Son of man, then shall ye know that I am he, and that I do nothing of myself; but as my Father hath taught me, I speak these things.

John 14, 10

Believest thou not that I am in the Father, and the Father in me? the words that I speak unto you I speak not of myself: but the Father that dwelleth in me, he doeth the works.

1. John 4, 4 - 6

Ye are of God, little children, and have overcome them: because greater is he that is in you, than he that is in the world.

They are of the world: therefore speak they of the world, and the world heareth them.

We are of God: he that knoweth God heareth us; he that is not of God heareth not us. Hereby know we the spirit of truth, and the spirit of error.

The Faith that moves Mountains

Mark 11, 22 - 25

And Jesus answering saith unto them, Have faith in God. For verily I say unto you, That whosoever shall say unto this mountain, Be thou removed, and be thou cast into the sea; and shall not doubt in his heart, but shall believe that those things which he saith shall come to pass; he shall have whatsoever he saith.

Therefore I say unto you, What things soever ye desire, when ye pray, believe that ye receive them, and ye shall have them.

And when ye stand praying, forgive, if ye have ought against any: that your Father also which is in heaven may forgive you your trespasses.

James 2, 20

But wilt thou know, O vain man, that faith without works is dead?

Romans 10, 17

So then faith cometh by hearing, and hearing by the word of God.

Hebrew 11, 1

Now faith is the substance of things hoped for, the evidence of things not seen.

Matthew 9, 29

According to your faith be it unto you.

John 7, 37 - 38

In the last day, that great day of the feast, Jesus stood and cried, saying, If any man thirst, let him come unto me, and drink. He that believeth on me, as the scripture hath said, out of his belly shall flow rivers of living water.

Hebrews 3, 14

For we are made partakers of Christ, if we hold the beginning of our confidence stedfast unto the end.

Ephesians 3, 20

Now unto him that is able to do exceeding abundantly above all that we ask or think, according to the power that worketh in us.

*We,
the Labourers in the Name of
Jesus Christ*

*

*A Message -
not only to the Apostles,
but also to us*

Matthew 9, 36 - 38

But when he saw the multitudes, he was moved with compassion on them, because they fainted, and were scattered abroad, as sheep having no shepherd.

Then saith he unto his disciples, The harvest truly is plenteous, but the labourers are few; Pray ye therefore the Lord of the harvest, that he will send forth labourers into his harvest.

Luke 10, 1 - 9

After these things the Lord appointed other seventy also, and sent them two and two before his face into every city and place, whither he himself would come.

Therefore said he unto them, The harvest truly is great, but the labourers are few: pray ye therefore the Lord of the harvest, that he would send forth labourers into his harvest. Go your ways: behold, I send you forth as lambs among wolves.

Carry neither purse, nor scrip, nor shoes: and salute no man by the way. And into whatsoever house ye enter, first say, Peace be to this house. And if the son of peace be there, your peace shall rest upon it: if not, it shall turn to you again.

And in the same house remain, eating and drinking such things as they give: for the labourer is worthy of his hire. Go not from house to house.

And into whatsoever city ye enter, and they receive you, eat such things as are set before you; and heal the sick that are therein, and say unto them, The kingdom of God is come nigh unto you.

*The Promise
of an Answer to Prayer*

John 14, 12 - 13

Verily, verily, I say unto you, He that believeth on me, the works that I do shall he do also; and greater works than these shall he do; because I go unto my Father.

And whatsoever ye shall ask in my name, that will I do, that the Father may be glorified in the Son.

Matthew 16, 19

And I will give unto thee the keys of the kingdom of heaven: and whatsoever thou shalt bind on earth shall be bound in heaven: and whatsoever thou shalt loose on earth shall be loosed in heaven.

*A Reminder to the Readers
to live a Life
according to their Calling*

Ephesians 4, 1 - 6

I therefore, the prisoner of the Lord, beseech you that ye walk worthy of the vocation wherewith ye are called, with all lowliness and meekness, with longsuffering, forbearing one another in love; endeavouring to keep the unity of the Spirit in the bond of peace.

There is one body, and one Spirit, even as ye are called in one hope of your calling; one Lord, one faith, one baptism, one God and Father of all, who is above all, and through all, and in you all.

*A Request
regarding your Behavior
towards one Another*

Ephesians 4, 25 - 32

Wherefore putting away lying, speak every man truth with his neighbour: for we are members one of another.

Be ye angry, and sin not: let not the sun go down upon your wrath:

Neither give place to the devil.

Let him that stole steal no more: but rather let him labour, working with his hands the thing which is good, that he may have to give to him that needeth.

Let no corrupt communication proceed out of your mouth, but that which is good to the use of edifying, that it may minister grace unto the hearers.

And grieve not the holy Spirit of God, whereby ye are sealed unto the day of redemption.

Let all bitterness, and wrath, and anger, and clamour, and evil speaking, be put away from you, with all malice:

And be ye kind one to another, tenderhearted, forgiving one another, even as God for Christ's sake hath forgiven you.

John 16, 33

These things I have spoken unto you, that in me ye might have peace.

In the world ye shall have tribulation: but be of good cheer; I have overcome the world.

Register

(1) Jesaja 40, 3
(2) Jesaja 53, 4 - 7
(3) Matthew 7, 29
(4) Jesaja 53, 4
(5) 3. Mose 13 - 49; 14, 2 - 32
(6) Luke 13, 28 - 29
(7) Matthew 22, 16
(8) 1.Kings 17, 23
(9) Matthew 10, 6
(10) Matthew 12, 30; Luke 11, 23
(11) Matthew 10, 42
(12) Matthew 6, 14
(13) Joel 4, 18; Sacharia 14, 8; Hesekiel 47, 1 - 12
(14) 4. Mose 27, 17; Hesekiel 34, 1 - 6
(15) Sacharia 8, 16
(16) Psalm 4, 5

Thanks and Inspiration

To this wonderful Project I was inspired by

The International School of Ministries

on which I just stared my Studies when the Idea to this Book came to me. The Lectures of the first Semester already touched me so deeply and found such Resonance inside of me, that I could finish this work very quickly - which basically contains the Lectures of the second Course of the first Semester.

The International School of Ministries teaches in many different Languages and builds on inspiring Teachers and Preachers from all Continents. This School offers to every Seeker not just a Guideline, but a deep Understanding of what the real Believe in our Lord Jesus Christ really contains, what it includes and to what it enables.

May God strengthen many more People in their Believe through the International School of Ministries and let them find Jesus in their Hearts.

ISOM Bible School

www.isom.org

About the Author:

www.antonia-katharina.de

www.bolonka-zucht.de

www.light-in-time.com

Youtube Kanal:
Antonia Katharina
aus dem Alten Jagdhaus

More Books of Antonia Katharina Tessnow

The Books of the Bible as separate, single Books in big Writing

Why the books of the Bible as separate singles? The reason is as simple as practical: Most of the time, the Bible in its entirety has a very small writing and is, therefore, hard to read. Even if the publication itself is as big as possible and the writing still hardly decent, it is practically impossible to carry around all day, ever since it is so heavy.

But the books of the Bible, published as single books, allows the writing to be nice and big and therefore easy to read. Instead of carrying a heavy, big book around, you can choose one book of your liking, light enough to put in every pocket and easy to read. This way you can read the Bible wherever you like. In other words: The translators made the Bible available, this version makes it possible to easily read it.

Additionally, the single and easy-to-read versions of the single, biblical books can serve as an entry into the most important book of all times. Also the different books can be given away as a present to friends, family and loved ones. The easy-to-read version of the Bible is not only perfect for all those, whose hearts the message of salvation already reached, but also for all those who did not yet dare to approach the Bible and possibly felt overwhelmed by the volume and length of it.

The message of the Holy Scriptures can be of great help and support, give confidence, bring hope, comfort you, show sympathy and give consolation, especially during times, when we need hope and consolation so very much.

Whoever is seeking for the way home should know, that it is always open and there for us. This way is shown and can be found through the Bible. By making the decision to open up for the message of the Holy Scriptures, many people, throughout centuries, have found salvation, safety, hope and peace. And that is true up to this day.

Writing, Format, Layout:
Antonia Katharina Tessnow

www.antonia-katharina.de

> *This Project is available*
> *in German and English*

Signs, Wonders and Miracles

in the Bible

*Testimonies from the
Old and New Testament*

And Jesus looking on them, saith:
'With men it is impossible;
but not with God:
for all things are possible with God.'

Mark 10, 27

This Publication offers a complete Compilation of all the Signs, Wonders and Miracles of the Bible. May this small Book bestow Faith, Hope and the firm Belief, that with God indeed all Things are possible.

I will praise and give Thanks to the LORD
with all my Heart
and speak of all thy marvelous Miracles.

Psalm 9, 2

Jesus' Love for Animals

Christian Inspirations from the Gospel of the Holy Twelve

Jesus Christ did not only teach us love for our humanly brothers and sisters, but also for our loyal, loving and tenderhearted companions, the animals.

The excerpts from the Gospel of the Holy Twelve, also known as the

Gospel of the Nazarenes

allow deep insights into the commands of our Savior, that is to confront our brothers and sisters, the animals, with love and treat them with full compassion. To everyone, who hopes to find orientation and to step safely through life: it is absolutely worth to align your being based on the teachings and commands of Jesus Christ, for he is and has always been the way.

Furthermore, a short attachment gives some understanding about the philosophy of other religions and writers, who also clearly confess their love of animals.

Holy Night
Silent Night

1943. It is Christmas. All around the world, children write diaries to somehow cope with the unbelievable experiences they are send through during wartimes and turmoil. The slightly older sister of Antonia Katharina`s mother is 9 years old when she describes the events of one single night through her childish eyes. A destiny that leaves deep impressions on ones soul and won`t leave anyone untouched.

A wonderful reminder of the peaceful times we are allowed to live in today.

Antonia Katharina Tessnow is the daughter of a former East Prussian Family who came to Germany after World War I. Her grandparents settled in Berlin but had to flee the city together with their children after their apartment building was bombed and completely destroyed during the last year of World War II. They returned many years later to Berlin, but even though Antonia Katharina was born there, she never felt at home in this city. Today she lives in the countryside of Mecklenburg-Vorpommern.

Madras
Magic of the Palm Leafs

This Book is available in English and German

The Palm Leaf Library - Thousands of years old and an unsolved secret until today. The mystery of this place is the key subject of 'Madras'. The true story evolves around one of the greatest secrets of mankind.

I have been there. I left my small hometown near Berlin and discovered a legend which says, that every life story is written on a palm leaf; every life story? No, but the live story of all those people, who will undergo the long travel to one of the libraries and search for it. That is what I have done.

And this is, what I have found.

People who have read this book:

'A fascinating book. Whoever wants to find the answer to the question: How many lives do we have? will find it here.'

Günther Prinz, Managing Director and Chief Editor of 'Bild', Germany.

'So there is my entire life written on a Palm Leaf in Madras! This book completely changed my understanding of time and space.'

Fritz Bloomberg, Ex-Vicepresident Burda Press, New York

'Mind blowing! The ideal book for everybody who wants to learn about the unbelievable truth behind our existence.'

Gregor Tessnow, Germany

Author of the bestseller and the script of 'Knallhart'

Ebenfalls von der Autorin erhältlich:

Heilbehandlungen für Dich und Dein geliebtes Tier

*Erinnere Dich
an Deine verborgenen Fähigkeiten*

Bolonka Zwetna

*Von der Empfindsamkeit der Hundeseele
und der Liebe, die sie schenkt*

Kommunikation mit Tieren

ein Essay

Die Botschaft der Tiere

Der Weg zurück zu uns selbst

Ein Wegweiser durch unsere Zeit

Augen auf beim Welpenkauf

*Wissenswerte Tipps aus der Bolonka Zwetna
Hundezucht aus dem Alten Jagdhaus*

Der Hund -
Das unbekannte Wesen

Was Sie tun können,
damit Ihr Hunde Sie liebt

*Ein Leitfaden zur Eingewöhnung
des Hundes in ein neues Heim*

Celtic Spirit

*Eine Reise in die Tiefen
zeitloser keltischer Weisheit*

HAIR

Alles über alternative Haarpflege

Sternenstaub am Horizont
oder
Breakable - Zerbrechlich
der Fall

zwischen Selbstwert und Vernichtung

Breakable - Zerbrechlich

Der Skandalroman aus Mecklenburg

Nichts geschieht umsonst auf dieser Welt
der Fall
Breakable - Zerbrechlich
die Anhänge

Tattoo – Laser – Cover Up

Wenn der Traum zum Albtraum wird

Weiß Du, was Du mit Dir trägst?

*Eine Entscheidungshilfe
für Tattoo und Motiv*

Stille Nacht, Heilige Nacht

Erinnerungen an einen Heiligen Abend
in den letzten Tagen des zweiten Weltkriegs

eine Kurzgeschichte

Diese Geschichte
liegt in deutscher und Englischer Fassung vor.

Winston

Eine Pferdebuch-Trilogie für Jugendliche

*Der große Sammelband
mit allen 3 Bänden*

Ein Fohlen erblickt die Welt

Die große Show

Nichts ist unmöglich

Copyright of the Original by

Antonia Katharina Tessnow

ALL RIGHTS RESERVED. No part of this book may be reproduced in any form or by any electronic or mechanical means including information storage and retrieval systems without permission in writing from the publisher, except by reviewers who may quote brief passages in a review.